Name: ___________________

UPPERCASE HANDWRITING PRACTICE

A B C D E F G

H I J K L M N

O P Q R S T

U V W X Y Z

LOWERCASE HANDWRITING PRACTICE

a b c d e f g

h i j k l m n o

p q r s t u v

w x y z

ALPHABET PROFESSIONS

Directions: Practice writing the profession in the space provided.

A is for
Astronaut

Astronaut

Astronaut

ALPHABET PROFESSIONS

Directions: Practice writing the profession in the space provided.

B is for
Beekeeper

Beekeeper

Beekeeper

ALPHABET PROFESSIONS

Directions: Practice writing the profession in the space provided.

C is for
Chef

Chef Chef

Chef Chef

ALPHABET PROFESSIONS

Directions: Practice writing the profession in the space provided.

D is for
Dentist

Dentist

Dentist

ALPHABET PROFESSIONS

Directions: Practice writing the profession in the space provided.

E is for
Engineer

Engineer

Engineer

ALPHABET PROFESSIONS

Directions: *Practice writing the profession in the space provided.*

F is for
Farmer

Farmer

Farmer

Trace the Letters

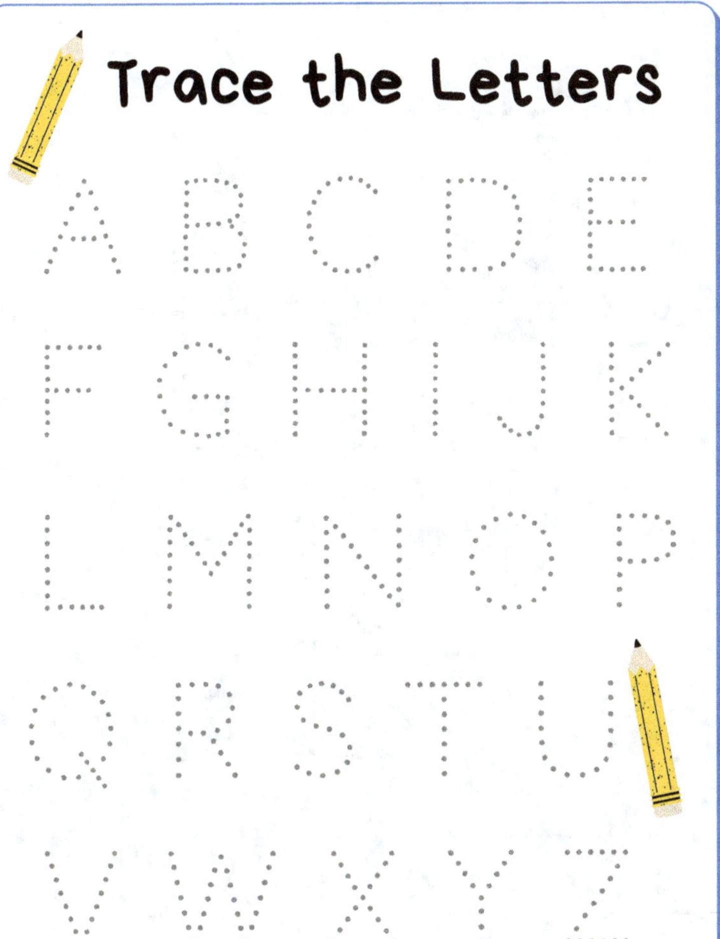

ALPHABET PROFESSIONS

Directions: Practice writing the profession in the space provided.

G is for

Geologist

Geologist

Geologist

ALPHABET PROFESSIONS

Directions: Practice writing the profession in the space provided.

H is for
Hairstylist

Hairstylist

Hairstylist

ALPHABET PROFESSIONS

Directions: Practice writing the profession in the space provided.

I is for
Illustrator

Illustrator

Illustrator

ALPHABET PROFESSIONS

Directions: Practice writing the profession in the space provided.

J is for
Judge

Judge

Judge

ALPHABET PROFESSIONS

Directions: Practice writing the profession in the space provided.

K is for
Karate Instructor

Karate

Instructor

ALPHABET PROFESSIONS

Directions: Practice writing the profession in the space provided.

L is for
Lifeguard

Lifeguard

Lifeguard

ALPHABET PROFESSIONS

Directions: Practice writing the profession in the space provided.

M is for
Musician

Musician

Musician

ALPHABET PROFESSIONS

Directions: Practice writing the profession in the space provided.

N is for
Newscaster

Newscaster

Newscaster

ALPHABET PROFESSIONS

Directions: Practice writing the profession in the space provided.

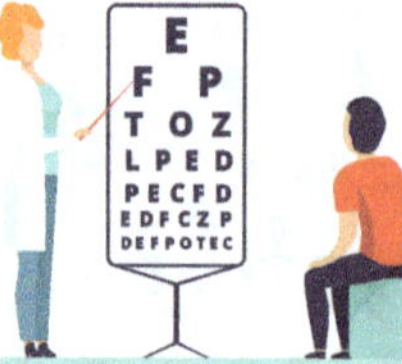

O is for
Optician

Optician

Optician

ALPHABET PROFESSIONS

Directions: Practice writing the profession in the space provided.

Q is for
Quilter

Quilter

Quilter

ALPHABET PROFESSIONS

Directions: Practice writing the profession in the space provided.

R is for
Receptionist

Receptionist

Receptionist

ALPHABET PROFESSIONS

Directions: Practice writing the profession in the space provided.

S is for
Scientist

Scientist

Scientist

ALPHABET PROFESSIONS

Directions: Practice writing the profession in the space provided.

T is for

Teacher

Teacher

Teacher

ALPHABET PROFESSIONS

Directions: Practice writing the profession in the space provided.

U is for

Umpire

Umpire

Umpire

ALPHABET PROFESSIONS

Directions: Practice writing the profession in the space provided.

V is for
Veterinarian

Veterinarian

Veterinarian

ALPHABET PROFESSIONS

Directions: Practice writing the profession in the space provided.

W is for
Writer

Writer

Writer

ALPHABET PROFESSIONS

Directions: Practice writing the profession in the space provided.

X is for
X-Ray Technician

X-ray Technician

X-ray Technician

ALPHABET PROFESSIONS

Directions: Practice writing the profession in the space provided.

Y is for
Yoga Instructor

Yoga Instructor

Yoga Instructor

ALPHABET PROFESSIONS

Directions: Practice writing the profession in the space provided.

Z is for
Zookeeper

Zookeeper

Zookeeper

ABC UPPERCASE APPLES

Practice your uppercase letter writing in the apples below. When
finished color the apples that contain vowels.

ABC LOWERCASE APPLES

Practice your lowercase letter writing in the apples below. When
finished color the apples that contain vowels using the color green.

COUNTING APPLES

Practice your number writing by tracing the numbers 1-15 in
the apples below. When finished color the apples.

FARM ANIMALS

PRACTICE WRITING THE FOLLOWING WORDS.

cow

sheep

goat

hen

pig

mouse

rooster

horse

bull

dog

cat

DIRECTIONS: TRACE THE WORDS AND NUMBERS BELOW.

DIRECTIONS: TRACE THE WORDS AND NUMBERS BELOW.

COLOR 2 STARS

CIRCLE THE 2'S

1	3	2
4	2	1
2	1	8
7	5	1
2	1	4

DIRECTIONS: TRACE THE WORDS AND NUMBERS BELOW.

CIRCLE THE 3'S

1	3	2
4	2	1
2	1	8
7	5	1
2	1	4

DIRECTIONS: TRACE THE WORDS AND NUMBERS BELOW.

COLOR 4 STARS

CIRCLE THE FOURS

1	3	2
4	2	1
2	1	8
7	5	1
2	1	4

DIRECTIONS: TRACE THE WORDS AND NUMBERS BELOW.

CIRCLE THE 5'S

1	3	5
4	2	1
3	1	5
7	5	1
2	9	4

DIRECTIONS: TRACE THE WORDS AND NUMBERS BELOW.

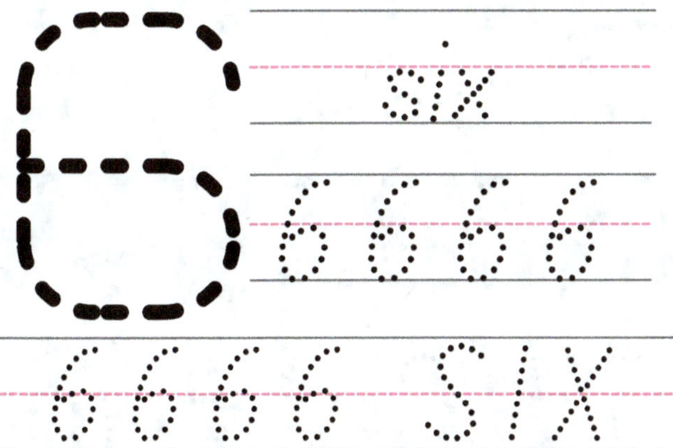

COLOR 6 STARS

CIRCLE THE 6'S

6	3	5
4	6	1
7	4	2
7	6	1
7	2	4

DIRECTIONS: TRACE THE WORDS AND NUMBERS BELOW.

CIRCLE THE 7'S

7 7 5
4 6 1
7 4 7
9 6 1
7 9 4

DIRECTIONS: TRACE THE WORDS AND NUMBERS BELOW.

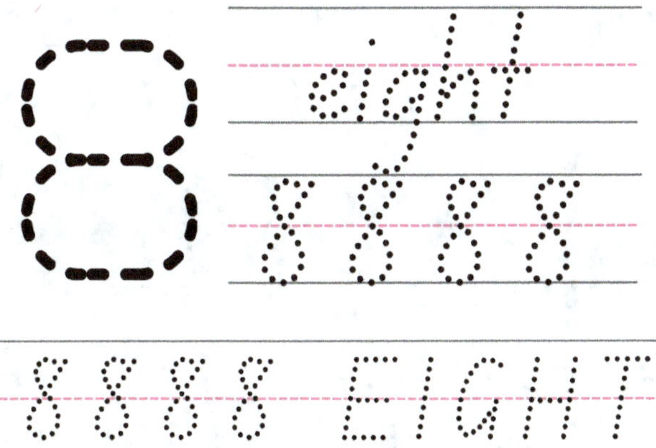

DIRECTIONS: TRACE THE WORDS AND NUMBERS BELOW.

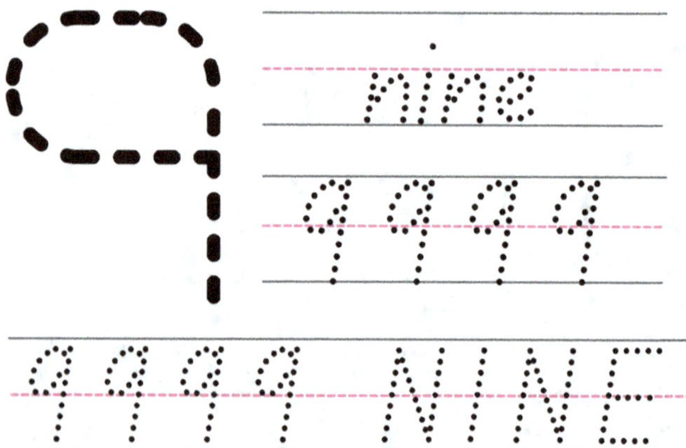

CIRCLE THE 9'S

8   7   5
7   6   9
9   8   7
6   0   1
4   9   2

MONTHS OF THE YEAR
HANDWRITING PRACTICE

January

February

March

April May

June July

August

September

October

November

December

ABOUT MY COMMUNITY
HANDWRITING PRACTICE

My Town

My state

My country

My school

My Teacher

WORKERS IN MY COMMUNITY
HANDWRITING PRACTICE

firefighter

doctor

police officer

dentist

mail carrier

TRANSPORTATION

PRACTICE WRITING THE FOLLOWING WORDS.

DIRECTIONS: PRACTICE WRITING EACH LETTER IN THE SPACE PROVIDED.

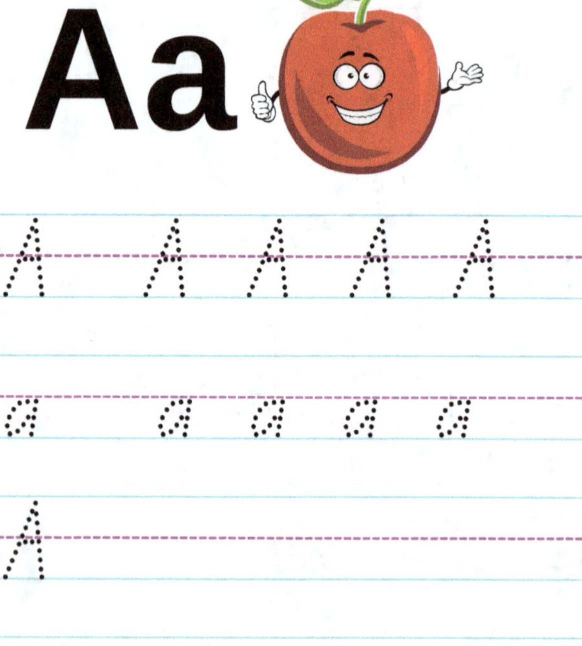

DIRECTIONS: PRACTICE WRITING EACH LETTER IN THE SPACE PROVIDED.

Bb

DIRECTIONS: PRACTICE WRITING EACH LETTER IN THE SPACE PROVIDED.

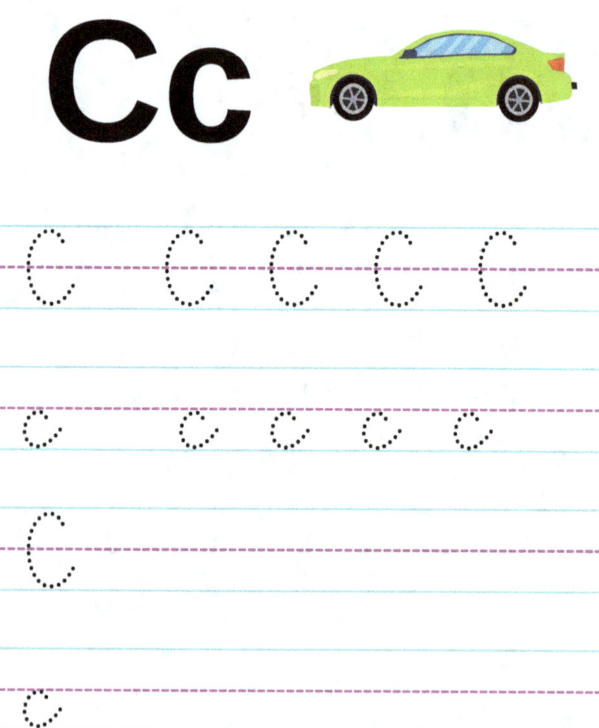

DIRECTIONS: PRACTICE WRITING EACH LETTER IN THE SPACE PROVIDED.

Dd

D D D D D D

d d d d d

D

d

DIRECTIONS: PRACTICE WRITING EACH LETTER IN THE SPACE PROVIDED.

DIRECTIONS: PRACTICE WRITING EACH LETTER IN THE SPACE PROVIDED.

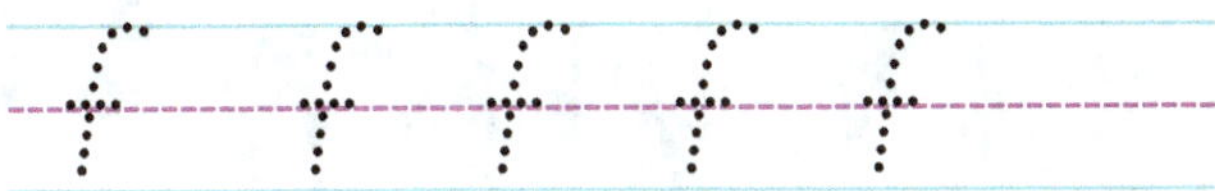

DIRECTIONS: PRACTICE WRITING EACH LETTER IN THE SPACE PROVIDED.

DIRECTIONS: PRACTICE WRITING EACH LETTER IN THE SPACE PROVIDED.

DIRECTIONS: PRACTICE WRITING EACH LETTER IN THE SPACE PROVIDED.

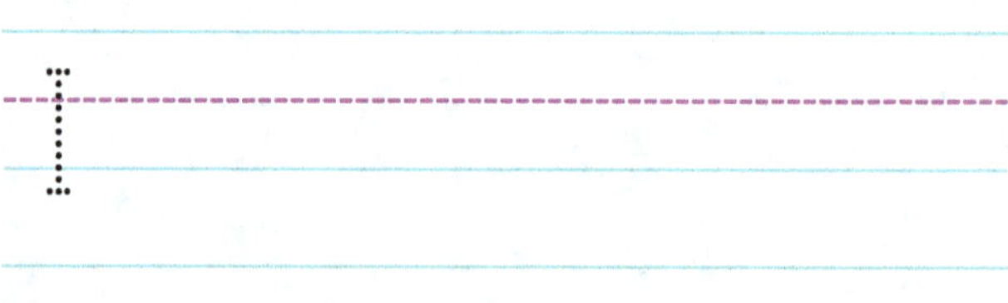

DIRECTIONS: PRACTICE WRITING EACH LETTER IN THE SPACE PROVIDED.

DIRECTIONS: PRACTICE WRITING EACH LETTER IN THE SPACE PROVIDED.

DIRECTIONS: PRACTICE WRITING EACH LETTER IN THE SPACE PROVIDED.

DIRECTIONS: PRACTICE WRITING EACH LETTER IN THE SPACE PROVIDED.

DIRECTIONS: PRACTICE WRITING EACH LETTER IN THE SPACE PROVIDED.

Nn

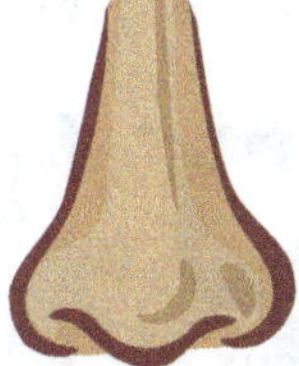

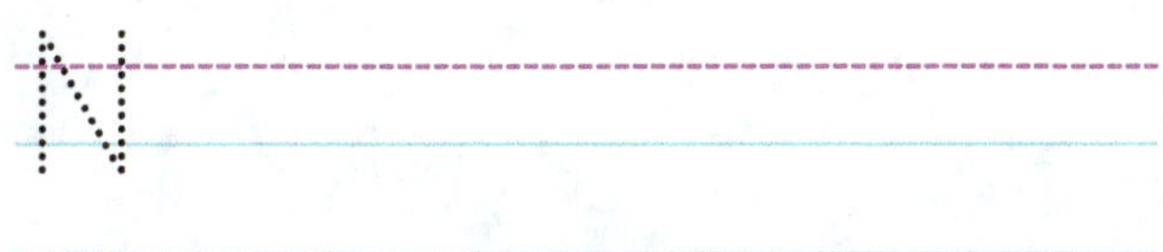

DIRECTIONS: PRACTICE WRITING EACH LETTER IN THE SPACE PROVIDED.

Oo

DIRECTIONS: PRACTICE WRITING EACH LETTER IN THE SPACE PROVIDED.

Pp

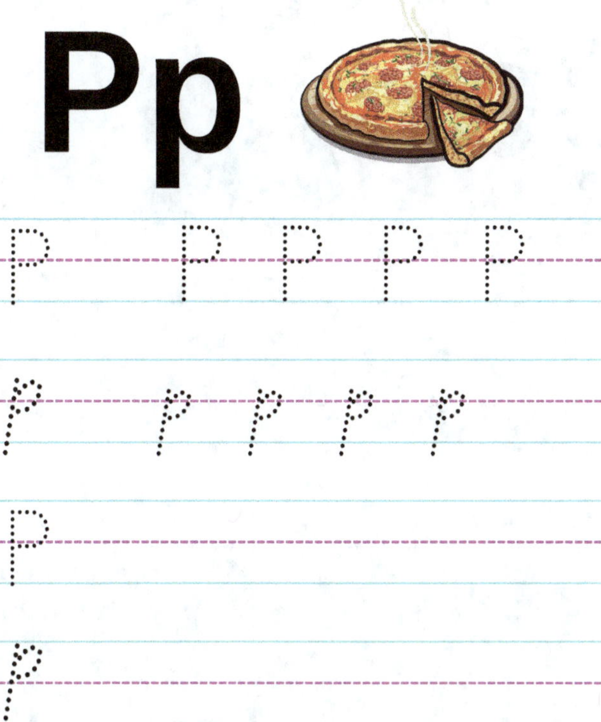

DIRECTIONS: PRACTICE WRITING EACH LETTER IN THE SPACE PROVIDED.

Qq

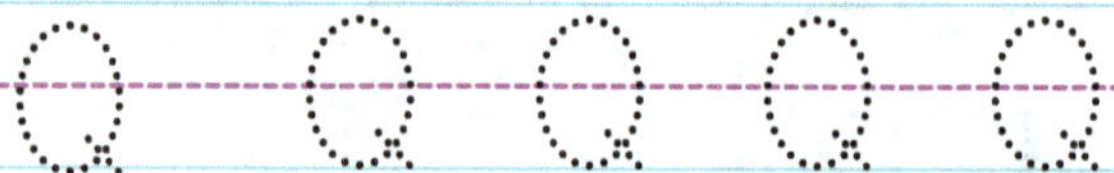

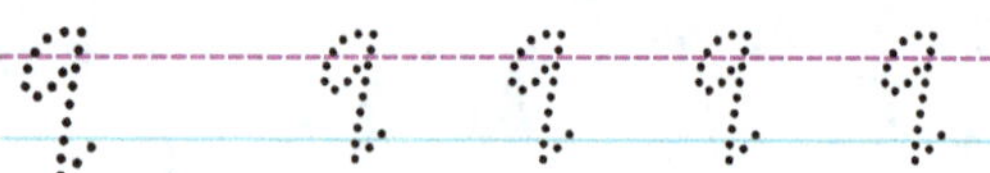

<table><tr><td>NAME</td><td>DATE</td></tr></table>

DIRECTIONS: PRACTICE WRITING EACH LETTER IN THE SPACE PROVIDED.

Rr

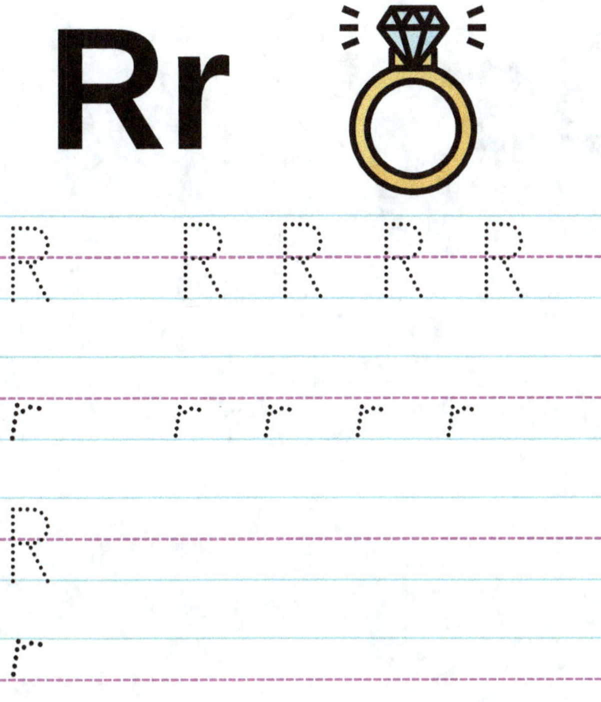

DIRECTIONS: PRACTICE WRITING EACH LETTER IN THE SPACE PROVIDED.

DIRECTIONS: PRACTICE WRITING EACH LETTER IN THE SPACE PROVIDED.

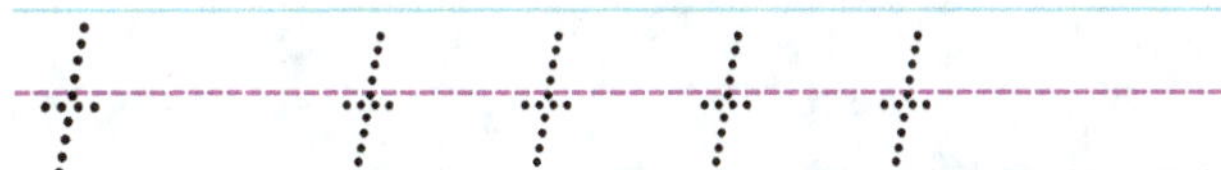

DIRECTIONS: PRACTICE WRITING EACH LETTER IN THE SPACE PROVIDED.

DIRECTIONS: PRACTICE WRITING EACH LETTER IN THE SPACE PROVIDED.

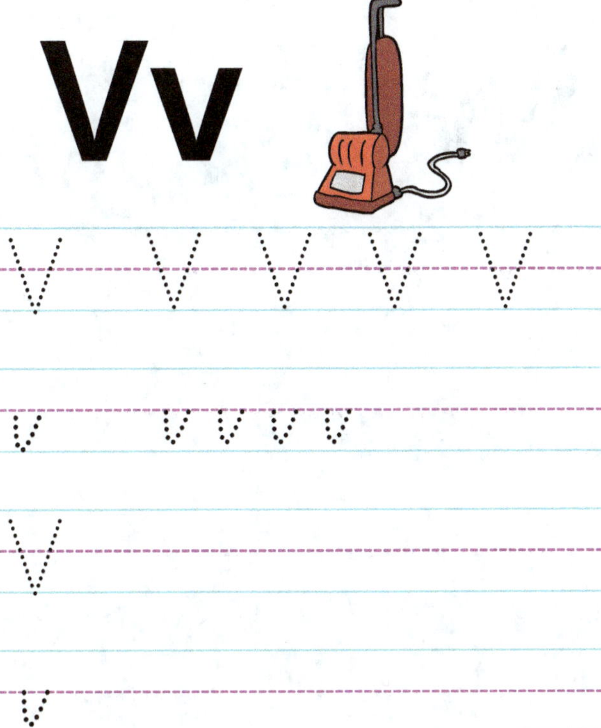

DIRECTIONS: PRACTICE WRITING EACH LETTER IN THE SPACE PROVIDED.

DIRECTIONS: PRACTICE WRITING EACH LETTER IN THE SPACE PROVIDED.

DIRECTIONS: PRACTICE WRITING EACH LETTER IN THE SPACE PROVIDED.

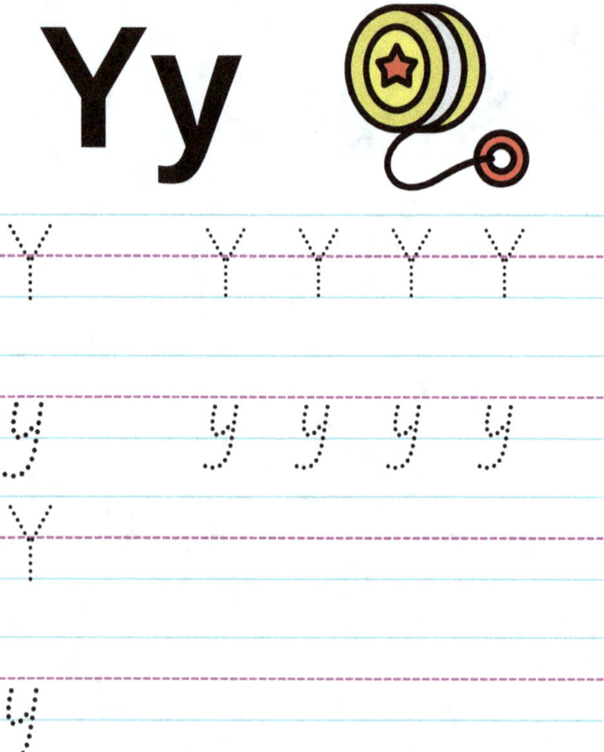

DIRECTIONS: PRACTICE WRITING EACH LETTER IN THE SPACE PROVIDED.

Zz

Z Z Z Z Z

z z z z z

z

z

Name:
Date:
I can write my name